100% UNOFFICIAL

JONAS BROTHERS

A MUST-HAVE GUIDE FOR 'SUCKERS' OF THE ICONIC POP SIBLINGS

Malcolm Mackenzie

DEAN

First published in Great Britain in 2020 by Dean,
an imprint of Egmont UK Limited,
2 Minster Court, 10th floor, London, EC3R 7BB
www.egmont.co.uk

Written by Malcolm Mackenzie
Designed by Ian Pollard

100% Idols: Unofficial Jonas Brothers © Egmont UK Limited 2020

ISBN 978 1 4052 9797 4

70967/001
Printed in Italy

Egmont takes its responsibility to the planet and its inhabitants very
seriously. We aim to use papers from well-managed forests run by
responsible suppliers.

JONAS BROTHERS

A MUST-HAVE GUIDE FOR 'SUCKERS' OF THE ICONIC POP SIBLINGS

Malcolm Mackenzie

CONTENTS

The Jonas Brothers are loved very MUCH!

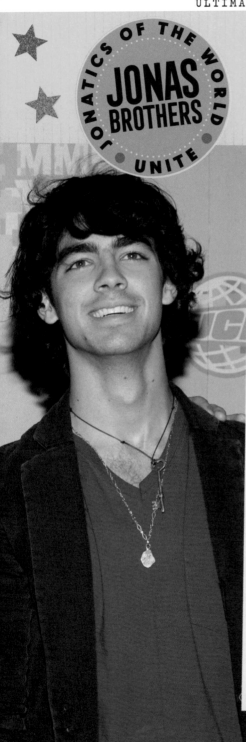

JONATICS OF THE WORLD
JONAS BROTHERS
UNITE

6 The brother of all comebacks

8 Jonas timeline

10 2005-2007: In the beginning

14 16 things you need to know about Nick

16 Nick Jonas: Solo star

18 The Jonas numbers

20 Making music

22 2008-2010: Mega stardom

26 16 things you need to know about Kevin

28 Kevin Jonas means business

30 7 essential Jonas Brothers videos

32 The Jonas lovers

34 2011-2012: A little break

36 Rocking with Disney

38 16 things you need to know about Joe

40 Joe Jonas: DNCE DNCE DNCE

42 Good sports

44 Lights, camera, acting

46 2013: Comeback and split

48 Joe's hair

50 10 things we learned from *Chasing Happiness*

52 Jokers brothers

54 9 essential Jonas Brothers bops

56 Nick's suits

58 2019- ...?: Comeback kings

62 Think you know the Jo Bros?

THE BROTHER OF ALL COMEBACKS

When the Jonas Brothers returned in 2019, the world lost its tiny mind.

The Jonas Brothers reforming couldn't have come at a better time. The world needed a bit of cheering up, but the return of three once goofy boys from New Jersey hit the sweet spot more than anyone could've anticipated. With the confidence only time can bring, the brothers were suddenly everywhere, seeming happier, more chilled and playful than ever. They produced fun, engaging content that made other pop stars seem boring by comparison and they looked incredible.

The reason the Jonas Brothers' comeback was initially so surprising is that it didn't need to happen. Most boybands get back together because not much else is going on, they miss performing and the money is lovely. But individually, the Jonas Brothers were doing incredibly well, which makes the fact they wanted to put the band back together even more special. They missed each other, they wanted to heal the wounds brought about by the split and wanted to spend their days creating music and playing it together.

Another thing that makes the Jonas reunion completely different is the fact that they didn't wait too long to do it. The brothers are still young and in their prime and just as hot and cool as anyone in the pop charts. If they'd waited ten years, it might have been an exciting nostalgic moment but also a bit like a bunch of dads trying to reclaim their youth. As it is, the Jonas Brothers are at the peak of their powers separately and together. They are still hugely relevant in the current pop climate – everyone is talking about them, their songs are on the radio and they keep racking up YouTube views and plays on streaming platforms from new fans and old.

To give you some idea about how popular the Jonas Brothers are right now you only have to look at the social media stats of other boyband members who got back together with their groups. Kevin Jonas, for example, has more Instagram followers than Nick Carter (Backstreet Boys), Jordan Knight (New Kids on The Block), Gary Barlow (Take That), Shane Filan (Westlife) and Ronan Keating (Boyzone) combined.

Nick, Kevin and Joe are not just a reformed band of brothers, they are a bona fide super group. Long may the happiness continue.

● Kevin is born.

● Joe is born.

● Nick is born.

● Nick releases his debut album *Nicholas Jonas* and first-ever single *Dear God*.

1987 〉 1989 〉 1992 〉 2002 〉 2004 〉

● Nick appears in the *Beauty and The Beast* musical.
● Joe appears in Baz Luhrmann's *La Bohème* musical.

JONAS

A lot has happened to these brothers.

Here's all the tea in a handy timeline.

● Joe Jonas releases his solo album *Fastlife*.

● Release the single *Pom Poms*.
● The Jonas Brothers split.

2010 〉 2011 〉 2012 〉 2013 〉 2014 〉

● *Camp Rock 2: The Final Jam* comes out.
● Nick Jonas and the Administration release their only album.

● Kevin and wife Danielle star in the E! TV show *Married to Jonas*.

● Nick releases his second album *Nick Jonas* and the single *Jealous*.
● Kevin is a contestant on *Celebrity Apprentice*.
● Kevin's first child Alena is born.

- Release debut album *It's About Time*.
- *Mandy* is a hit on MTV.
- Start working with Disney.

- Release the album *A Little Bit Longer* and singles *Burnin' Up* and *Lovebug*.
- *Camp Rock* airs on the Disney Channel.

2005 » 2006 » 2007 » 2008 » 2009

- The Jonas Brothers form and sign with Columbia Records.
- Nick is diagnosed with type-1 diabetes.
- The Jonas Brothers' debut single *Mandy* is released.

- Sign with Hollywood Records.
- Release the album *Jonas Brothers* and singles *Hold On* and *S.O.S.*
- Appear on *Hannah Montana* episode *Me and Mr Jonas and Mr Jonas and Mr Jonas*.

- Release the album *Lines, Vine and Trying Times* and singles *Tonight* and *Paranoid*.
- Nominated for a Grammy Award.
- Kevin marries Danielle Deleasa.
- The boys star in their own 3D concert film.
- The first episode of *Jonas* the TV show airs on the Disney channel.

TIMELINE

Hands down the best boyband.

- Kevin's second child Valentina is born.
- Nick releases his third album *Last Year Was Complicated*.

- Nick marries Priyanka Chopra.

2015 » 2016 » 2017 » 2018 » 2019

- Joe forms DNCE and has a smash hit with *Cake By The Ocean*.

- Nick stars in the movie *Jumanji: Welcome to the Jungle*.

- The band announce their reunion.
- Release the album *Happiness Begins* plus singles *Sucker* and *Cool*.
- Release *Chasing Happiness* documentary on Prime Video.
- Release the memoir: *Blood*.
- Joe marries Sophie Turner.

2005-2007
IN THE BEGINNING

From church to schools to the Disney Channel – The Jonas Brothers' steady rise to the top.

EARLY BLESSINGS

The Jonas boys grew up in the New Jersey town Wyckoff with their mother, a sign-language teacher, and their church pastor father. The brothers would join their music-loving father, Kevin Jonas senior, onstage in church to perform songs that their dad had written.

BROADWAY BABY

Despite being the youngest, it all started with Nick. Nick would break into song, as kids do, and one day a woman suggested he get a manager, because obviously the kid had pipes. Pretty soon Nick, or Nicholas as he was called then, was performing on Broadway playing parts such as Tiny Tim in *Scrooge* when he was eight, Chip in *Beauty and The Beast* when he was nine and Gavroche in *Les Miserables* when he was just ten.

YOU'RE NICKED

By the time he was 12, Nick had released his first solo album called *Nicholas Jonas*, but Joe and Kevin were not completely out of the picture. They co-wrote and sang on some of the songs, so unsurprisingly when the suggestion was made by record company Columbia Records to form a group, it seemed like an excellent idea.

JONAS ASSEMBLE

The Jonas Brothers formed in 2005, releasing their debut single *Mandy* in December. The song, written by Nick, Kevin and Joe, was featured on the Nickelodeon show *Zoey 101* but it failed to chart. The album *It's About Time* came out in 2006 and featured two prominent Busted covers – *That's what I Go To School For* and *Year 3000*, which they released as a single that got to number 31 in the US singles chart selling over a million copies. Kerching!

In the beginning there was hair wax and gel – a lot of it.

DISNEY: THE RESCUERS

Despite a modest amount of success, Columbia Records dropped the band. Luckily Hollywood Records, a subsidiary of Disney, were there to snap them up. Disney put the boys to work recording a version of *Poor Unfortunate Fools* for a special edition of *The Little Mermaid* soundtrack, they put out a *Pirates of the Caribbean* track and perfomed the theme tune to the Disney cartoon *American Dragon: Jake Long.*

SOS SPELLS SUCCESS

Disney knows a thing or two about success so when they released the Jonas Brothers' second album *The Jonas Brothers* it was a worldwide hit, cracking the top ten of the UK and US charts. *SOS*, their first single in Europe, provided the brothers with their first truly global hit. It sold two million copies and three well-mannered boys who could really rock were on their way.

The Dickensian street urchin look, thankfully didn't last.

2005-2007
IN THE BEGINNING

The band were very briefly called Sons of Jonas.

Nick released his first album when he was 12. His debut single was called *Dear God*.

Joe made his Broadway debut in Baz Luhrmann's production of *La Bohème* in 2002 – the same year Nick was in the musical *Beauty and The Beast*.

When the first Jonas Brothers album came out Nick was 13, Joe was 16 and Kevin was 17.

Kevin starred in a number of TV commercials when he was a kid including one for E-Brain, a weird electronic 'companion' – a bit like a lo-fi Alexa.

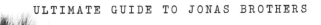

The Jonas Brothers were so talented and driven that it was simply a matter of time before they would get their big break ...

Kevin described early Jo Bro sound as "Music on Red Bull".

The first ever Jonas Brothers song was written on the daily commute between New Jersey and New York at the suggestion of their dad.

Ambitious from the start, the Jonas Brothers released three different videos with one continuing story for their debut single *Mandy*.

Upon release, *Mandy* became the number one requested video on the MTV show *TRL*.

The song that got the Jonas Brothers signed to Columbia was *Please Be Mine*.

FULL NAME:
Nicholas Jerry Jonas
BORN:
16 September 1992

16 THINGS YOU NEED TO KNOW ABOUT ...

NICK

Get to know the youngest brother in the band.

1 The first song he learned to sing was "If you're happy and you know it."

2 Nick weighs 163lbs (well he did in 2016).

3 He has a scar on his left middle finger from playing with a pocket knife – silly boy.

4 His biggest fear is flying.

5 Nick drives a cool 1960 Thunderbird Red convertible.

6 He credits his early start on Broadway for his work ethic, his love of performing and vocal stamina. "I think it was the best vocal training I could have had," he says.

7 He loves Italian food. What did you expect? The family comes from New Jersey.

8 Nick would love to write a Broadway musical.

9 His worst habit is checking his phone at the dinner table.

10 Nick was diagnosed with type 1 diabetes when he was 13. He lost about 23lbs in two weeks, his blood sugar was "off the charts," and he could have died. Nick has to live with the condition for the rest of his life, and although he has many tools to manage it, he admits that, "Every day there are moments that are challenging."

The *Pizza Girl* video is mouth-wateringly weird.

11 Nick's least favourite Jonas Brothers song is *Pizza Girl*.

12 Nick cannot whistle.

13 Wanna know if Nick Jonas is staying at a hotel? Try asking for Nigel Greenberg, it's an alias he's used in the past. Shhh.

14 Some of the artists Nick likes to listen to are The Beatles, Shania Twain, Drake and The Doobie Brothers.

15 Nick's favourite boardgame is Monopoly.

16 The comedian that makes him laugh the hardest is Kevin Hart.

Nick learned his stage craft early on.

NICK JONAS
SOLO STAR

Nick was a star from the moment he sang for his mum's friends in the local hairdresser.

BREAKING CHAINS

Nick's first proper solo single wasn't a big hit in the UK, but it did fairly well in the US and established Nick as a solo artist to be reckoned with. The video was also something of a revelation showing lil' Nicky all grown up in a ripped T-shirt, with a buzzcut, all muscles and stubb

A BIT OF ADMIN

Perhaps inspired by Selena Gomez and The Scene, instead of going solo straight away, in 2009 when the Jonas Brothers were still huge, Nick eased himself into life without Joe and Kev by creating a new band, Nick Jonas and the Administration. He brought together an amazing bunch of musicians who'd played for Prince and the album *Who I Am* got to number three in the US.

THE FUTURE LOOKS GOOD

Demi Lovato is virtually part of the Jonas family so when the *Future Now* tour was announced with Demi and Nick, fans were chuffed to bits. The shows, a combination of solo numbers and duets, kicked off on 29 June 2016 in Atlanta. A *Camp Rock* reunion happened in Washington when Joe joined the pair onstage to perform the songs *Gotta Find You* and *This Is Me*.

Nick and Demi ha
been close since
were teenagers.

JEALOUS

Jealous is the highest charting hit of any Jonas release in the UK, getting to number two. It sold three million copies in the US. It was epic. It was not without controversies however. The lyric: "I turn my chin music up," caused much mishearing and discussion and is still written as "Cheek, music ..." on iTunes. Nick confirmed in an interview that "chin music" is when you have major attitude and presumably jut your chin.

THINGS GET COMPLICATED

Nick Jonas' most recent solo album *Last Year Was Complicated* was packed with amazing songs and got to number two in the main US chart. Singles *Close* with Tove Lo and *Bacon* with Ty Dolla$ign were catchy sparse-sounding sophisticated pop tunes, and album tracks like *Champagne Problems* and *Under You* were as good as anything Nick had released, but the record didn't have any massive hits. Tsk – people don't know what's good for them.

When Nick Jonas performed a dodgy guitar solo with Kelsea Ballerini at an awards show in 2016, he joked about it, saying it was due to a 'huge brain fart'.

THE JONAS
NUMBERS

1+1+1 adds up to something very special indeed.

$500,000

The amount Kevin helped to raise for charity on *Celebrity Apprentice* in the US.

34

The number of *Jonas/Jonas LA* episodes there were.

21

The number of weeks the Jonas Brothers songs have spent inside the UK top 40.

2 million

The number of singles *Sucker* sold in America alone.

Camp Rock 3?

Joe Jonas says he would make a third *Camp Rock* movie if all the other cast were up for it and it got an R rating, which means everyone under 17 has to be accompanied by an adult to see it.

280,000

The number of tickets Demi and Nick sold for their *Future Now* tour.

980 years

The amount of time till the year 3000.

1410

The name of a line of shoes Nick launched with the brand Creative Recreation in 2017.

34th

Sucker was the 34th single to debut in the Billboard Hot 100 at number one.

7+ million

Number of Instagram followers the Jonas Brothers have.

$800,000

The amount Nick Jonas and Priyanka Chopra's wedding is said to have cost.

(818) 748-8887
The telephone number the Jonas Brothers set up for fans to call and leave messages back in 2009.

1 month
The length of time Miley Cyrus says she cried after Nick broke up with her.

13
The age both Nick and Kevin were when they had their first kiss. Joe was 16.

500
The number of times Danielle said yes (approximately according to Kevin) after he proposed to her.

YES! YES! YES!
YES! YES! YES!
YES!

20
Frankie Jonas turns 20 in the year 2020. Follow his Insta @franklinjonas.

10%
The amount of their earnings they reportedly gave to charity in 2007.

92 Toyota Camry
The car the Jonas family used to ferry the kids to and from New York for their Broadway shows as kids.

2 minutes 33 seconds
The length of *S.O.S*, the Jonas Brothers' shortest ever single.

Jonas maths: Joe says four, Nick says two – what does it all mean?

MAKING MUSIC

The Jonas Brothers aren't just an assemblage of ace genes and lustrous hair, they are crazy talented!

KEY PLAYER
Nick plays four musical instruments: guitar, bass guitar, drums and piano.

"I started writing songs with my dad when I was really young and knew really early it would be something that was important for me in my life."

NICK JONAS

BEAT IT!
Nick was singing from the age of three, but the first instrument he learned to play was the drums.

CIRCUS JONAS
Kevin doesn't just play guitar, he sings back up, co-writes the songs and in the early days did backflips on a trampoline – while continuing to play his guitar!!!

PERFORMANCE ART
Although Joe plays guitar, he usually concentrates on his electric and energetic stage performance.

The Jonas Brothers co-wrote all the singles on Demi Lovato's debut album.

BOY OH BOY
The Jonas Brothers are not the sort of boyband that sing other people's songs sat on stools, and maybe dance a bit. They. Do. Everything. Themselves. (As part of a team – obviously).

2008-2010
MEGA STARDOM

For a time the Jonas Brothers were on the radio, TVs, computers and cinemas screens – oh happy days.

THE DREAM IS REAL

The Jonas Brothers became such hot properties that in May 2008 they launched their very own Disney Channel reality TV show *Jonas Brothers: Living The Dream*. The 27 episodes followed the boys on tour, going behind the scenes as they went sky diving, learnt to drive, did school work, played sports, and were generally a fun time.

The trio were an unstoppable force.

NUMBER ONE

In the summer of 2008, the brothers released their third album *A Little Bit Longer* and it went to number one in America selling over half a million copies in a single week. A year later they released their fourth album *Lines, Vines and Trying Times*, which they described as a musical diary, and that too went to the top of the US chart.

TOUR, TOUR, TOUR

The Jonas Brothers are as much a rock group as they are a boyband, so when success hit they went on tour, after tour, after tour. They basically never stopped. The *When You Look Me in the Eyes* tour

in 2008 was their first as a well-known band. That was followed by the *Burning Up* tour which was a whopper, raking in over $20 million, and that was swiftly followed by their third headline tour in less than two years – the excitingly named *World Tour 2009*.

The Jonas Brothers were nominated for Best New Artist at the 2009 Grammy Awards.

GOOD CHOICE

The Jonas Brothers were so massive that they won Favourite Music Group two years running at the Nickelodeon Kids' Choice Awards. As for the Teen Choice Awards, well what didn't they win? Between 2008 and 2010 the Jonases won a whopping 15 awards – little brother Frankie even won one for his role in their TV show, *Jonas L.A.*

BURNIN' UP THE SINGLES CHART

Till *Sucker*, *S.O.S.* was the Jonas Brothers' biggest hit in the UK, but *Burnin' Up* gave them their biggest hit across the pond, reaching number five in June 2008 and going on to sell approximately two million copies. The song remains one of their most popular songs to this day. The retro sound of the single *Lovebug* didn't fare so well, but the Jonas Brothers bounced back into the US top ten with the atmospheric rock out *Tonight*. Nick loved the song as much as the fans and re-recorded a version of *Tonight* for his album *Who I Am* with his band The Administration.

SCREEN TIME

It's a good job the Jonas Brothers are so cute because for a three year period they were never off screens. After their Disney docuseries, they were given their very own scripted TV show *Jonas,* where they played fictionalised versions of themselves, they made two *Camp Rock* movies, released a live 3D concert film and even had their own Nintendo DS video game based on their Disney TV show – oh brother.

The Jonas brothers pick up one of many Teen Choice awards.

2008-2010
MEGA STARDOM

Number one albums, sell out tours, awards, waxworks, fandemonium – the Jonas Brothers are AWESOME!

The Jonas Brothers were sculpted in wax by Madame Tussauds. The boys are now frozen in time in 2009 forever.

In 2008 the Jonas Brothers revealed that the Beckham children were such big fans that Victoria said they might form their own band: The Beckham Brothers - if only.

When fans discovered where the brothers lived they would just turn up, knock on the door and sometimes if the door was open, let themselves in.

The Jonas Brothers released their own line of clothing inspired by the preppy wardrobe of the characters from their Disney channel TV show *Jonas*.

Kevin, Joe and Nick play animated flying cherubs in the movie *Night at The Museum 2* and sing *More Than A Woman* by the Bee Gees and *My Heart Will Go On* by Celine Dion.

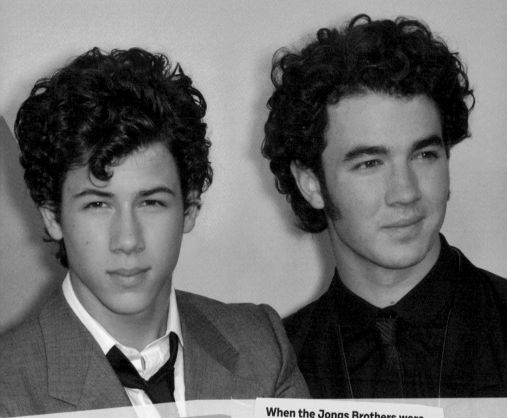

Nick Jonas passed his driving test on the same day they shot the cover of the album *Lines, Vines and Trying Times*.

When the Jonas Brothers were invited to the White House for a night honouring Beatles legend Paul McCartney, they performed *Drive My Car* – at Macca's request.

Jonas Brothers were ahead of the curve when it came to K-Pop. The boys invited Korean girl group Wonder Girls to join them on their 2009 tour – four years before BTS even launched.

The strangest fan encounter the brothers had was when a girl asked Joe to hit her. When he wouldn't she gave him a thump and ran away.

Most boybands say they wouldn't date a fan, but the Jonas Brothers regularly said they would – and indeed Joe did.

Joe is sometimes embarrassed by the old Jonas Brothers – specifically his flat-ironed hair, squeaky voice and *Camp Rock* dance moves.

FULL NAME:
Paul Kevin Jonas II
BORN:
5 November 1987

16 THINGS YOU NEED TO KNOW ABOUT ...

KEVIN

Big brother Kevin is the mysterious one, well he was ...

1 Kevin's first name is actually Paul. PAUL!?!

2 Paul - sorry - Kevin taught himself to play the guitar when he was sick at home and got bored of watching TV.

3 When he was a kid Kevin says he was "a total nerd."

4 Kevin took Joe to a tattoo parlour when he was 14 years old, and his parents were not pleased.

5 Kevin was the first to take off his purity ring.

6 Kevin's homemade remedy to get rid of styes in your eyes is to put cold tea bags on them.

7 Ever the entrepreneur, Kevin once said that his dream job would be the CEO of Starbucks.

8 Kevin leaves his wife Danielle a stack of love letters when he goes on tour, one for every day.

Kevin's kids can watch dad perform onstage and in videos like *Sucker*.

9 He's the dad of two little girls, Alena and Valentina.

10 Nick is godfather to Kevin's youngest daughter Valentina, who was initially quite jealous of Nick's wife Priyanka.

11 Before the reunion, Kevin thought his kids might never have the opportunity to see him perform.

12 Kevin's 2007 straight and spikey hairdo took an hour and a half to create.

13 He is somewhat jealous of Nick's enormous shoe collection.

14 Kevin was called as a witness to give evidence in the FIFA corruption trial. He was asked to confirm that a Paul McCartney concert had taken place in Argentina. Random.

15 One of Kevin's worst habits is throwing clothes everywhere.

16 According to Nick and Joe, Kevin has the uncanny ability to seek out the lens of any camera and give it a direct look.

This hairstyle took ages to get right.

KEVIN JONAS
MEANS BUSINESS

In the early days it seemed like Nick was the grown-up, sensible one. Nah, it's Kevin.

MARRIED TO JONAS

When the Jonas Brothers started pursuing solo projects, it gave Kevin some free time for the first time and he jumped at the chance to create a programme around his family life. The show pulled back the curtains of Kevin and Danielle's home, but did not just focus on the Jonases and their careers, it also introduced viewers to Danielle's instantly likeable family. The executive producer of the show was The Kardashians creator himself, Ryan Seacrest.

Kevin also appeared on the reality TV show Man Caves.

KEVIN TAKES ON TRUMP

Before he was president of the United States, Donald Trump was a TV personality on the US version of *The Apprentice* and Kevin was a contestant. Kevin however did not make it very far in the show. After taking the initiative to be project manager he was fired when his team "Vortex" lost, and he tried "to out-think" Donald Trump. Kevin admitted that he learned a lot about himself filming the show. "I'm a risk taker," he said, "I just want to do whatever it takes to do the best I can."

BIG BUSINESS

It's no surprise Kevin was on *Celebrity Apprentice*, he's a mini-mogul in the making. Instead of blowing his Jonas Brothers money on diamond loo seats, he invested wisely in numerous business ventures, so while his brothers explored separate solo paths, Kevin found ways of working where he wasn't always the product.

Danielle and Kevin: the orginal Jonas love story.

TECHIE MAX

Because he knows a thing or two about engaging with an audience, one of Kevin's many business ventures is an influencer marketing company called The Blu Market. "I've always had a passion for the tech industry. It was a no brainer," he explained. Kevin also launched a mobile gaming company called Phillymack that created games for Demi Lovato and his brother's band DNCE as well as a delicious food location app, Yood.

Kevin's company created *Zombarazzie*: a game where you help Demi Lovato defeat hoardes of zombie paparazzi.

PLAYING HOUSE

These days you don't just have to fill your house with the music of the Jonas Brothers, you can actually get Kevin Jonas to build your house. Kevin is part owner of the construction firm Jonas/Werner Fine Custom Homes. The company specialises in designing and building beautiful mansions in New Jersey and he even popped up as the contractor on *The Housewives of New Jersey*, consulting with one of the wives, Kathy Wakile, on her new home.

Kevin Jonas
Singer/Kathy's Contractor

7 essential JONAS BROTHERS VIDEOS

There's a reason they have four million subscribers on YouTube, and it's because of this ...

YEAR 3000

1 This trip to the future is a major journey to the past. It's by no means a 'good' video, but for pure nostalgia it can't be beaten. The boys are so fresh-faced and enthusiastic, and the song is so much fun, that it's easy to overlook a time machine that is in actual fact an old sofa cushion and people of the future that are just girls in pink party wigs.

S.O.S.

2 The song is called S.O.S. and the video is set on a giant ocean liner, like the Titanic – genius. Instead of the voyage across the sea ending in disaster the boys' love lives sink without a trace. Nick is ousted in favour of friends, Kevin is dumped by a cryptic and cruel text message, and Joe's girl is cheating on him with what appears to be a ten year old. Worse things DO happen at sea.

LOVEBUG

3 A sophisticated mini-movie that sees the boys playing adorable 1950s geeks in knitted tank tops and thick-framed specs taking a whizz around on a boat, before serving up some major entertainment as the band at an old school dance in spiffy white tuxedos. It's pretty, romantic and they look excellent done up to the nines. If the 35+ million YouTube views are anything to go by, this is a fan fave.

BURNIN' UP

4 Nick Jonas as a teenage James Bond. Sold. Done. Everyone go home. What? There's more? Joe as a Miami Vice cop replete with white suit and moustache, kung-fu master Kevin kicking ass and flying, an actual cameo from Selena Gomez and someone doing a pretty ropey impersonation of Taylor Swift. Classic Jonas. It was nominated for video of the year at the MTV awards but didn't win. #robbed.

FIRST TIME

5 The last video the Jonas Brothers made before they split in 2013 is a rough montage of Vegas shenanigans but it says so much about where the band were at the time. Nick is working on music alone in his hotel room, Kevin is loved up with Danielle, and Joe is seen getting the drinks in and shaving his head. It was supposed to be uplifting, but knowing what we now know, it's bittersweet.

SUCKER

6 When three become six. Fans can get jealous, catty and downright trollsome when it comes to the WAGs of their musical heroes, but the Jonas Brothers and each of their beautiful wives cause nothing but joy. It was especially heart-warming to see Danielle, Sophie and Priyanka serving us fierce fashions and flawless face alongside their husbands in *Sucker* – a song that's ALL about THEM.

COOL

7 It's the 80s in Miami and the Jonas Brothers are what? COOL. Strutting up the street in zoot suits, rocking out on the beach, demanding the attention of attractive young women and blue-rinse pensioners. This video sees the Jonases at their playful best, hamming it up and really enjoying themselves. Nick is buried up to his neck, Kevin is plagued with parrots and they even sing submerged in a basin of water.

THE JONAS LOVERS

Who wouldn't snap up these men? Meet the women that put a ring on it and call themselves Mrs Jonas.

JOE AND SOPHIE

Joe's romance with *Game of Thrones*' Queen of the North Sophie Turner is a totally modern affair. Joe DM'ed Sophie on Instagram, they met up, they hung out, and two and half years later were getting married by an Elvis impersonator in Vegas. They also had a crazy-romantic ceremony in the south of France, because, y'know, they're celebs.

Nick was actually the first person to hint that the couple were dating, captioning a pic of the pair on Insta: 'These two,' heart-emoji.

NICK AND PRIYANKA

Not many guys marry a woman ten years older than them, but that's exactly what Nick did and that's one of the things that makes the relationship between Nick and Bollywood actress Priyanka Chopra so special: love is love and when it hits, it knows no boundaries.

Nick and Priyanka tied the knot twice, having both a Christian and a Hindu ceremony. The wedding celebration in India lasted four days.

THE ONES THAT GOT AWAY

GIGI HADID

Before she dated Zayn Malik, supermodel Gigi Hadid was all about Joe Jonas, who she romanced for five months. Before that she dated Cody Simpson. Shawn Mendes had better watch out.

OLIVIA CULPO

The former Miss America and Nick were inseparable for two years, then they separated. It was an amicable break-up. The two sat down with a bottle of champagne and toasted their time together. So grown up.

KEVIN AND DANIELLE

Despite living in New Jersey not far from the Jonas family home, Danielle Deleasa met Kevin on holiday in the Bahamas way back in 2007 and they kept in touch after the vaycay. The best scene in the Jonas doc *Chasing Happiness* is of Kevin on the phone to Danielle inviting her to her first Jonas Brothers show.

In December 2009, Kevin and Jewellery designer Danielle were married in a fairytale wedding in a castle on Long Island in the snow – dreamy.

2011-2012
A LITTLE BREAK

After five years, the Jonas Brothers juggernaut began to slow down as the brothers explored personal projects.

In 2011, Nick appeared on Broadway in *Hairspray the Musical*. He played Link Larkin, the role made famous by Zac Efron in the movie.

At the end of 2011, a Gagesque new Jonas Brothers song *Dance Until Tomorrow* was leaked, but it was never released.

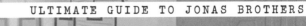

In March 2012, Kevin tweeted a video of Joe and Nick making music, but fans had to wait another year to hear the fruits of their labour.

The Jonas Brothers started a tour to promote an album called *V* that never was. Fans got to hear new songs *Let's Go* and *The First Time* and *Wedding Bells*.

In 2012, Nick starred in the Broadway show *How To Succeed in Business Without Really Trying*, Kevin launched his reality TV show *Married to Jonas*, and Joe considered his options after releasing his solo debut album *Fastlife*.

During this period the Jonas Brothers, who in many ways had outgrown Disney, parted ways with the Disney owned label Hollywood Records.

ROCKING WITH
DISNEY

In the golden age of the Disney Channel, the Jonas Brothers were kings.

Miley knows how to party.

HANNAH MONTANA

The Jonas Brothers appeared on Miley Cyrus' mega-hit TV show *Hannah Montana* in August 2007 in an episode tiled *Me and Mr Jonas and Mr Jonas and Mr Jonas*. It aired right after *High School Musical 2* and was seen by over ten million people – the most watched episode of *Hannah Montana* ever, catapulting the brothers to massive fame. Miley and the Jonas Brothers performed the song *We Got The Party* together in the episode.

CAMP ROCK

When the Jonas Brothers appeared in the Disney Channel movie *Camp Rock*, a musical rom-com about a group of aspiring musicians, they were at the height of their fame and Demi Lovato was an unknown. After the film that all changed. Over eight million people tuned in to watch the film in June 2008 when it premiered – more than the original *High School Musical* film. Demi and the brothers would remain close from then on – some, (Joe!!!) closer than others.

Demi is almost one of the family.

JONAS TV

After *Camp Rock*, Disney jumped at the chance to give the brothers their own scripted TV show. *Jonas*, and the follow-up second season *Jonas LA*, were inspired by classic musical comedy TV hybrids like *The Monkees* and *The Partridge Family* as well as the knockabout laughs of The Beatles movies. Confusingly the characters have the same first names as the Jo Bros, but with the surname Lucas, and the band they're in is weirdly called JONAS. The show ran for two seasons on the Disney Channel between May 2009 and October 2010.

CO-STAR KISS-A-THON

Nick Jonas may be married now but he was very popular at Disney when he worked there dating Hannah Montana star Miley Cyrus and Selena Gomez while she was in *Wizards of Waverly Place*. If that wasn't weird enough, Joe dated Demi Lovato and Taylor Swift. People forget that Taylor appeared in both the Hannah Montana movie and the Jonas Brothers' own concert film.

Hot damn! Kevin treats Taylor Swift to a hot dog.

✳ ✳ ✳ ✳
CAMP ROCK 2

The original film did so well that of course there was a sequel. *Camp Rock 2: The Final Jam* saw the characters from the orginal movie facing off against a rival band camp and drew nearly eight million viewers, giving Disney another hit film. The made-for-TV movie aired in September 2010 and won the People's Choice Award for favourite family movie. Double bill anyone?

When the Jonas Brothers were cast in *Camp Rock* they weren't very well known and Joe had to audition multiple times before he got the part of Shane Gray.

FULL NAME:
Joseph Adam Jonas
BORN:
15 August 1989

16 THINGS YOU NEED TO KNOW ABOUT ...

JOE

Some totally random facts about the 2nd Jo Bro!

1 His fave Netflix binge is *Stranger Things*.

2 His choice of superpower would be to fly – but to somehow stay warm (he's given it some real thought).

3 Joe used to live in a 'haunted' or at least very freaky house. He moved.

4 He was the first Jonas to meet Kevin's future wife, Danielle.

5 Joe considered starting a band with his DNCE drummer Jack Lawless called Tic-Jack-Joe.

6 Joe has swum with sharks.

7 If you wanna catch Joe at a festival go to Coachella – he's been at least five times.

8 Joe has skinny-dipped, and found the experience "freeing".

9 He enjoys rummaging in vintage stores.

10 On his 21st birthday he had rather a bit too much to drink and fell down a flight of stairs.

11 If Joe is enjoying a big breakfast he'll have porridge, eggs, and sometimes even steak.

12 Miles Davis is Joe's favourite jazz musician.

13 Joe has a wicked sense of humour. He once pretended to have Chelsea Kane fired fom their TV show *Jonas LA*.

14 When they first came to the UK, someone gave the Jonas Brothers jellied eels. Joe ate two and felt sick for days.

15 He once admitted to fancying his third grade teacher, then he bumped into her and it was more than a bit awks.

16 When Joe comes to London he likes to visit Harrods and the swanky Ritz casino, but he also keeps it real with trips to Pizza Express.

Joe and Gigi Hadid at Coachella.

JOE JONAS

DNCE DNCE DNCE

It took Joe a while to find his feet, but once he started DNCE-ing everything fell into place.

THE LOST ALBUM

While Nick was administrating his musical independence in 2010, Joe was exploring his own sound. He made an album with the lead singer of respected indie rockers Rooney. The project had a retro 80s Hall & Oates vibe, with Joe delivering powerful vocals inspired by Freddie Mercury – but when he played the songs to his record company they were baffled and the songs were scrapped.

THE JNAS DNCER

Nick Jonas formed a band then went solo, Joe did the reverse – going solo, then deciding he wanted to be part of a gang again. Enter DNCE. The groovy four-piece are made up of bassist Cole Whittle, who was in the band Semi-Precious Weapons with *Cake By The Ocean* songwriter Justin Tranter, guitarist Jinjoo Lee who met Joe when she toured with The Jonas Brothers as part of Jordin Sparks band, and Jack Lawless who was The Jonas Brothers tour drummer and in actual fact Joe's roomie.

Solo Joe supported Britney on her *Femme Fatale* tour – LITERALLY.

FAST LOVE

Joe released his own solo album *Fastlife* in 2011, and although Joe thinks the record suffered from "too many cooks," it still

holds up to this day with solid Britney energy courtesy of producer Danja. *See No More* co-written with Chris Brown is an emotional banger, *Love Slayer* is an absolute corker and *Just In Love* is a propulsive funky floor-filler stacked with Justin Timberlake vibes – and the romantic video is just - phew.

FINDING HIS VOICE

Joe's career came full circle when in 2018 he stepped in as the fourth coach on *The Voice Australia*. Knowing a thing or two about struggling for success Joe found the experience rewarding saying that he enjoyed: "Working with artists that are wanting to work hard and are willing to soak up any knowledge that you might throw at them." Who wouldn't want JJ as their teacher?

CAKE AND EAT IT

DNCE's biggest hit *Cake by The Ocean* has over 800 million streams on Spotify – the most popular song of any Jonas release on that platform, but did you know the massive cake fight video was directed by Joe's then girlfriend, Gigi Hadid? Or that the song is a metaphor for canoodling, that arose after some slang got lost in translation with one of the Swedish songwriters?

Enjoy the big band stylings of solo Joe on the Hotel Transylvania 3 soundtrack – It's Party Time is pure Bublé brilliance.

GOOD SPORTS

Sometimes being competitive has its rewards, because the Jonas Brothers are FIT in more ways than one.

FOOTBALL
It might not be massive in the States, but since touring has made the Jonas Brothers borderline International, of course they're fans of the beautiful game.

GOLF
Kevin says playing golf keeps the Jonas Brothers sane when they're on tour because, "... nobody else is out there, just you and the course." Nick has been playing longest, but that doesn't stop his older brothers from trying to beat him.

RUNNING
Nick Jonas has said that he hates running, but he will make the exception if it's for charity. Here he's running a 5k with Joe to raise funds for the Special Olympics as part of the Jonas Brothers' own Change For Children Foundation.

TENNIS

From the pictorial evidence it's unclear if the Jonas Brothers actually know how to play tennis, but Kevin has enough enthusiasm to make any match 'interesting'.

BASEBALL

We have rounders and cricket in the UK, in the US they have baseball, and it's huge. If he could have any other job apart from being in show business Nick says he'd be a baseball player: he does look good in the uniform – they all do.

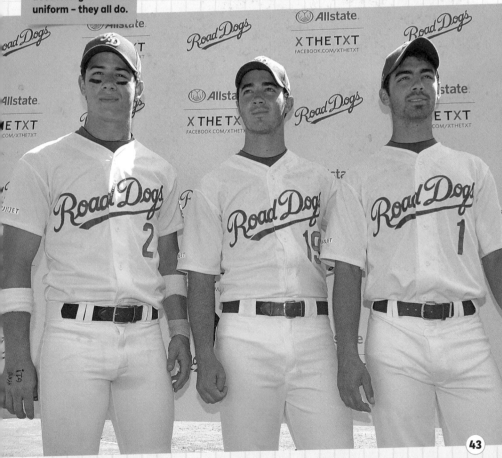

LIGHTS, CAMERA, ACTING

Where does Nick Jonas find the time? When he's not singing , touring or writing he's acting his socks off.

KINGDOM (2014-2017)

Fans saw a totally different side to quiet thoughtful Nick in the TV show *Kingdom*, where the singer played the part of a mixed martial arts fighter. The drama series ran for three seasons giving Nick the chance to really stretch his acting chops – not to mention his karate chops. Nick trained three times a day for the role, put on 15lbs of muscle and ate a whopping 4200 calories a day.

CAREFUL WHAT YOU WISH FOR (2015)

Nick's breakout big screen role was playing Doug Martin, a young guy who falls in love with a married woman with murderous results in *Careful What You Wish For*. The film gave fans and Hollywood the chance to see Nick carry a movie.

"The biggest thing I've learned is that you can't have any fear when you're acting. Any ounce of fear will show."
NICK JONAS

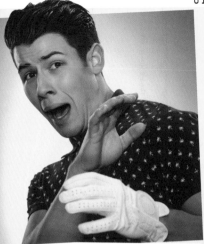

MIDWAY (2019)

Nick Jonas has followed in Harry Styles' hallowed footsteps to star in an all guns blazing epic war blockbuster. Like *Dunkirk*, *Midway* is about a real-life decisive moment in the Second World War, and despite being a very serious film, Nick, who plays a fighter pilot, looks like he could have come straight from the video of *Lovebug*. Too much handsome.

SCREAM QUEENS (2015)

Spoiler alert! As Boone Clemens in Ryan Murphy's *Scream Queens*, Nick Jonas played a frat boy with a love for golf who also happened to be a serial killer! He dressed in a red devil costume and faked his own death. It was a lot.

Nick has said that he would like an acting career like Mark Wahlberg – who also started out as a musician.

JUMANJI (2017, 2019)

Jonatics rejoice: Nick Jonas is now part of a movie franchise – *Jumanji*. In 2017 Nick starred with The Rock, Karen Gillan, Jack Black and Kevin Hart in the family action adventure film *Jumanji: Welcome to The Jungle* which went on to become the highest grossing movie in Sony history. Naturally there had to be a sequel, *Jumanji: The Next Level*, and lucky for Nick (and us) he's in it.

2013
COMEBACK AND SPLIT

It could have been so different, but sadly the first Jonas Brothers comeback was followed by a swift exit.

In April 2013, the Jonas Brothers returned with brilliantly bombastic and brassy brand new single *Pom Poms*.

Despite being catchy as hell with a super-fun stadium-filled video clip, *Pom Poms* barely troubled the charts on either side of the Atlantic.

It was a dark time for Jonatics when the band cancelled their tour and scrapped their fifth album titled *V*.

On 29 October 2013, the Jonas Brothers split up.

When they split, Nick said they were "closing a chapter," while Kevin left fans with hope saying, "it's over – for now."

As a parting gift, the brothers released a live album called *LiVe* that contained six new tracks that would have appeared on the *V* album.

When the band broke up, Nick was still only 21.

JOE'S HAIR

With a face this handsome you can get away with any hairstyle, well almost.

Joe Jonas has had more hairstyles than Kevin has had business ventures.

4 DECEMBER 2007
Before Joe embraced his natural curls he had a borderline obsession with hair straighteners.

20 AUGUST 2006
Short and spiky hair like a radish was all the rage in the early noughties. Sadly it suited no one.

AUGUST 13 2008
Here Joe is a couple of layers and highlights away from having a 'Rachel from Friends'.

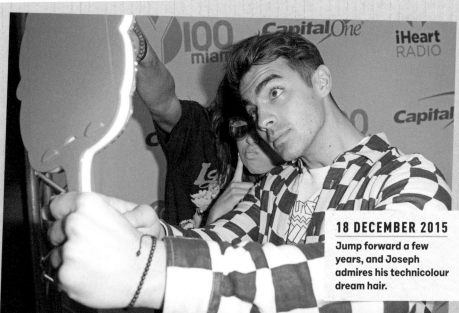

18 DECEMBER 2015
Jump forward a few years, and Joseph admires his technicolour dream hair.

19 MARCH 2016
When you dye your hair the colour of your face you run the risk of looking washed out. Thank goodness for those eyebrows.

27 AUGUST 2017
The adorable ruffle top is joined by luxurious Super Mario lip hair.

10 THINGS WE LEARNED FROM ...
CHASING HAPPINESS

The Amazon Studios documentary is packed with titbits. Here are some of the best.

1 Joe once chipped his tooth onstage during a show by shoving the mic too hard into his face.

2 Before the band, Kevin couldn't get a date, but after the Disney Channel played their video, everything changed.

3 Meeting Miley Cyrus and falling in love with her was the perfect 'a-ha moment' for Nick. After that he could suddenly write love songs.

4 Kevin Jonas senior invested $90,000 into the band – his life savings – and after Columbia dropped the band they were broke, their career seemed in doubt, they were ostracised by friends, their dad lost his job and they had to move house - yikes.

5 The moment the brothers realised they had 'made it' was when they came to perform a concert in Oklahoma and the traffic was terrible because of them. They had to helicopter into the show.

6 Joe predicted Kevin would marry Danielle in November 2007. They actually tied the knot on 19 December 2009. In an amazing moment of archive footage we see Joe and Nick feeding lines to Kevin while he's on the phone to Danielle and it's adorable.

7 Every time the Jonas Brothers released an album they would go to Virgin Megastore in Time Square New York to buy it – the second it came out at midnight. Every year the number of fans that showed up increased until it became a scrum of mayhem with 20,000 fans, fire engines and police.

8 They never said no. The boys said yes to every interview and meet and greet to the point of exhaustion. They were hard working because they knew how fleeting fame could be.

9 Nick's biggest regret was agreeing to make season two of the *Jonas* TV show. He thinks it stunted their growth and they couldn't evolve because of it.

10 Joe's proudest time was 2019 because it was the year he grew as a person and grew with his brothers. He also got married and had a number one record.

Things get personal and emotional in *Chasing Happiness.*

JOKERS BROTHERS

**You know the world is safe and sound
if the Jonas Brothers are goofing around.**

HOLD ONNNN!!!

PICK-UP ARTISTS
When tight jeans aren't quite enough, Nick and Kevin do everything they can to help Joe hit the high notes.

HOW YOU DOIN'?

POUT AND PROUD
If Nick Jonas wants a snog, he only has to ask – or pull this kissy-kissy face.

SHOCKED EMOJI
Is Kevin the joker of the Jonas Brothers? Nick certainly seems to think so.

YES, I HAVE FRESH BUNS.

WIENER TAKES IT ALL
Everybody calm down, chef Kevin has enough Jonas hot dogs to go round.

NUMBER ONE FAN
When things hot up, there's only one way to cool down: with Jonas Brothers fans. Kev is the coolest obvs.

SAY CHEESE-CAKE
When you've eaten as much cake by the ocean as Joe, you need to check for sprinkles and frosting before you take a selfie.

9 essential JONAS BROTHERS BOPS

Any JB playlist should include these bad boys.

MANDY

1 A power pop juggernaut that launched a gazillion Jonatics. For sheer exuberance Mandy is hard to beat. Despite being rough around the edges, this lo-fi thrashing ode to a shy girl called Mandy, who's almost too good to be true, is a fiesty little number that's so noisy it's hard to believe it ever passed as pop music for children. It's pretty punk even if it does reference S Club 7. Crank it up and annoy the cat.

HOLD ON

2 How many angsty teenagers in exam meltdown did this song help? Plenty. The first single from the Jonas Brothers' second album is an irresistible rockin' anthem with a message to stay strong no matter what life throws at you. Nick and Joe really sell the concept with pleading chorus squeals that literally crack with emotion – or maybe that's puberty.

S.O.S.

3 The perfect pop song about a failing teenage relationship with someone who has an annoying group of friends. We've all been there. Melodically it's so pure, like early Beatles it rocks along with a driving beat before exploding into super-catchy chorus and is finished in two and a half minutes – job done. Guess we'll just have to put it on again.

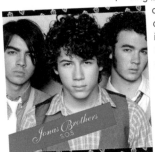

BURNIN' UP

4 The most successful Jonas single in America before *Sucker*, *Burnin' Up* entered the chart at number five, quite literally burning up the Billboard Hot 100. If the lyrics comparing fancying someone to falling into lava don't make you feel the heat then the funky guitar, sweet harmonies and infectious rhythms will. Someone open a window, it's getting mighty warm in here.

PARANOID

5 The Jonas sound expands into dramatic eighties rock that evokes the widescreen twangs of U2 in a song that explores a crippling modern affliction: anxiety. The first single from their fourth album was written with Cathy Dennis, who famously wrote *Toxic* for Britney Spears – she clearly knows how to write about psychological issues and make them pop!

SEND IT ON

6 Any song that features the Jonas Brothers, Miley Cyrus, Demi Lovato and Selena Gomez has to be worth 3.26 minutes of your time. Yes it might be a cheesy ballad but hearing these well-known voices blend together and belt out a positive message about the environment is a guilty pleasure. It has an *X Factor* winner's single feel and you can totally imagine someone singing it at Eurovision.

POM POMS

7 The Jonases first comeback, a clattering percussive celebration of the brothers at their wildest, should have been a hit. Maybe that was part of the problem, people weren't ready for the funk. They really let loose and go for it, producing some of their most passionate vocal deliveries. It almost makes you want to take up cheerleading – although we suspect "pom poms" are a metaphor for something, ahem, else.

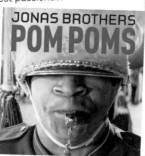

SUCKER

8 How on earth did the Jonas Brothers pull this off? Comeback track *Sucker* is not only the best Jonas Brothers song ever – it's one of the best songs of the decade. It literally is all singing and dancing with whistles and bells and harmonious harmonies, hand claps and the angelic Nicholas Jonas falsetto we never tire of hearing. It's a catchy, infectious mood enhancer and basically the best way you can spend three minutes.

ONLY HUMAN

9 Who knew that what we really wanted from the Brothers Jonas was reggae? The more you hear this slow burn track, the more you find to love from the tinkle of steel drums to the horns and Rhianna-like ad-libs. It's a mid-tempo low-key banger that has you on your feet and shoulder popping like you're on the Caribbean summer holiday of your dreams.

NICK'S SUITS

It's obvious that Nick Jonas has a flair for fashion, he especially loves a smart suit.

13 MAY 2010

After a rocky style start Nick Jonas slowly became the most fashionable man in pop. Check this slick three-piece suit from the Young Hollywood Awards.

24 FEBRUARY 2015

Nick looked dapper as hell in an irridescent olive green tuxedo jacket for the Elle Style Awards.

29 MARCH 2015

This perfectly tailored red check suit with a slim black tie is elegant while evoking the spirit of punk at the same time.

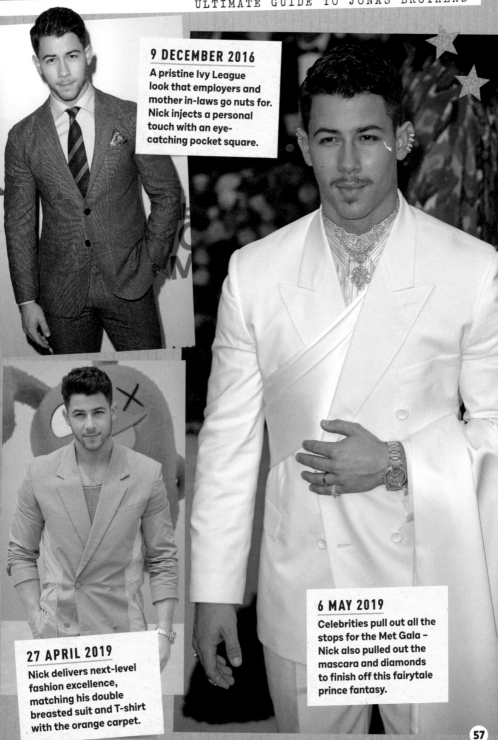

9 DECEMBER 2016

A pristine Ivy League look that employers and mother in-laws go nuts for. Nick injects a personal touch with an eye-catching pocket square.

27 APRIL 2019

Nick delivers next-level fashion excellence, matching his double breasted suit and T-shirt with the orange carpet.

6 MAY 2019

Celebrities pull out all the stops for the Met Gala – Nick also pulled out the mascara and diamonds to finish off this fairytale prince fantasy.

2019-...?

COMEBACK KINGS

We didn't know how much we needed the Jonas Brothers until they came back. Never leave us again boys.

SURPRISE!!!

On 28 February 2019, after six years of silence, the Jonas Brothers returned. A tweet from the official @jonasbrothers account announced a brand new single *Sucker* with the now familiar artwork of three colourfully-attired men strolling away from a balloon-strewn mansion. What followed was a sea of online screams and celebratory memes. The tweet now has over 200,000 likes.

BIGGER THAN EVER

Making a comeback deals heavily in nostalgia and typically fans care more about the classics than new music, but *Sucker* was massive! It went straight to number one in America, something no boyband had achieved in over a decade, not even One Direction. It was huge across five continents, getting to number one in Australia, Canada, Singapore, Lebanon and Latvia. It was their biggest hit ever in the UK, reaching number four. The album *Happiness Begins* went to number one in the US and number two in the UK.

The Jonases won their first VMA in 2019.

MTVICTORY

Until 2019 the Jonas Brothers had never actually won an MTV Video Music Award. That all changed with *Sucker* which beat Taylor Swift, Ariana Grande and Billie Eilish to win best pop video of the year. They also paid tribute to their home state of New Jersey at the show, performing *Sucker* inside local club the Stone Pony before taking things onto the Asbury Park boardwalk to blast out *Only Human*.

AMAZON PRIMED THEM

The Jonases started filming their Amazon documentary a year and a half before their comeback. The film was going to end highlighting their individual solo projects, but during filming they missed the old magic and got back together.

Car-cool karaoke.

CARPOOLS OF CROON AND SWOON

When celebs want to make an impact they often appear on a chat show. The Jonas Brothers took this method seriously, appearing on James Corden's *Late Late Show* four days in a row, just to make sure people got the message that they were back. Watching the trio belting out *Burnin' Up, Year 3000, When You Look Me In The Eyes, Lovebug* and *Sucker* for the first time in ages on *Carpool Karaoke* was an emotional watch. Tissues were definitely needed.

HAPPINESS PREVAILS

The boys did not want to dwell too much on bad feelings and get moody about what happened in the past – this comeback campaign was all about happiness. In case you couldn't tell, they released an album called *Happiness Begins*, put out a film on Amazon Prime called *Chasing Happiness* and took the *Happiness Begins* tour out on the road. Enjoy all of that lot and happiness is virtually guaranteed.

Colour blocking and Jonas rocking on the *Happiness Begins* tour.

COMEBACK KINGS

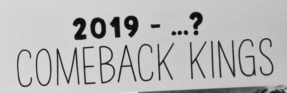

> *So much has happened since the boys returned, but now that they're back, we can't wait to see what they do next.*

The Jonas Brothers gave fans a surprise bonus track in the form of *Greenlight*, a song written by songwriter Able Heart for the reality competition TV show *Songland*. It went to number one on the US iTunes sales chart.

When the Jonas Brothers came back, all their back catalogue got an uplift with streams of *Burnin' Up*, *S.O.S.* and *Lovebug* increasing by over 300%.

The wives of the Jonas Brothers collectively call themselves the J-sisters. Fingers crossed for a collab.

The band obviously knew that they were coming back seven or eight months before they released *Sucker*, and keeping the secret was hard.

Joe and his wife Sophie were the most nominated couple at the 2019 People's Choice Awards. She was nominated for four awards and he for three.

To celebrate 25 years of *Friends*, the Jonas Brothers posted a re-cut of their *Sucker* video to the theme tune *I'll Be there For You* by the Rembrandts.

If anyone tells you that the Jonas Brothers aren't cool, they're wrong and here's the proof. Jay-Z was seen having a ball at one of their recent concerts and even went backstage to meet the guys. If it's good enough for Hova …

The Jonas Brothers have done a lot of press since their comeback, but the best photoshoot – hands down – was for *Paper* magazine where they hilariously recreated the cringiest family photos imaginable. Genius.

Nick describes the current Jonas music as a mash up of DNCE's funky side, Nick's punchy pop solo output combined with the classic rockin' Jo Bro sound.

THINK YOU KNOW THE JO BROS?

Take this quiz now. Don't be paranoid, you're gonna do great.

Test Your JB IQ

1 **What was the surname of the brothers in the Disney movie *Camp Rock*?**

A ☐ Green

B ☐ Gray

C ☐ Grant

2 **What was the surname of the brothers in the Disney TV show *Jonas*?**

A ☐ Spielberg

B ☐ Scorsese

C ☐ Lucas

3 **Which sport did Kevin love so much at school that he went to a camp dedicated to it.**

A ☐ Table Tennis

B ☐ Pole Vault

C ☐ Diving

4 **Which song is NOT on *Chasing Happiness*?**

A ☐ *Lonely*

B ☐ *Love Her*

C ☐ *Rollercoaster*

5 **The Jonas Brothers once had the cops called on them three times – why?**

A ☐ Partying too hard at Joe's stag do.

B ☐ Blasting out *Year 3000* over and over when it went top 40 in the Billboard chart.

C ☐ Skinny-dipping on a Caribbean holiday

6 **What did Nick Jonas say the slime at the Nickelodeon Kids' Choice Awards tastes like?**

A ☐ Bubblegum

B ☐ Yoghurt and oatmeal

C ☐ Apples and soap

7 **Which singer features on the Jonas Brothers song *Before The Storm*?**

A ☐ Miley Cyrus

B ☐ Taylor Swift

C ☐ Selena Gomez

8 **What is the Jonas Brothers' favourite thing to eat in hometown New Jersey?**

A ☐ Taylor ham and cheese breakfast sandwich

B ☐ Blake chipotle biscuit burger

C ☐ Monroe chilli hot dogs and slaw

9 **Joe and his wife Sophie have matching tattoos of what?**

A ☐ The house Stark sigil

B ☐ The Jonas Brothers logo

C ☐ Their dog Waldo

10 **Who was spotted wearing a Jonas Brothers T-shirt in July 2019?**

A ☐ Harry Styles

B ☐ Justin Bieber

C ☐ Shawn Mendes

ANSWERS

1B, 2C, 3B, 4A, 5A,
6A, 7A, 8A, 9C, 10B

8-10
Jonatic
Are you sure you're not
Frankie Jonas? You
seem to know an awful
lot about the boys from
Wyckoff. You can call
yourself a true fan,
congratulations
– you cool!

5-7
Jonapal
The Jonas Brothers are
important to you, but
so are other things. If
Joe forgets the lyrics
sometimes, you too
can be forgiven for not
knowing everything,
you're only human.

0-4
Jonawho?
Did you pick this book
up by accident? It's
good, right? You did
the quiz so maybe
there's hope for you yet.
Read it and take the
test again, don't be a
sucker.

CREDITS

Front cover: PICTURES: Image Press Agency / Alamy Images.

4-5: PICTURES: ZUMA / Alamy Images.

6-7: PICTURES: MediaPunch Inc / Alamy Images, ZUMA Press, Inc. / Alamy Images.

8-9: WORDS: Wikipedia, Allmusic.com, billboard.com, About.com, Refinery29.com. PICTURES: UPI / Alamy Images, Geisler-Fotopress GmbH / Alamy Images.

10-13: WORDS: MTV.com: Corey Moss, Playbill.com, Christianmusic.about.com: Kim Jones, Billboard.com: Gary Trust, PRnewswire.com, nicholasjonasbroadway.jimdo.com, music.monstersandcritics.com: Mikael Wood, Buzzfeed.com: Ehis Osifo, Insider.com: Meghan Cook. PICTURES: ZUMA Press, Inc. / Alamy Images, Featureflash Archive / Alamy Images, Everett Collection Inc / Alamy Images.

14-15: WORDS: MTV, WIRED, IGN, We Love Pop magazine, US Weekly. PICTURES: MediaPunch Inc / Alamy Images, Everett Collection Inc / Alamy Images, Bravo/NBC Universal, Hollywood Records Inc, Disney Music Group.

16-17: WORDS: Teenvogue.com: De Elizabeth, USAtoday.com, Wikipedia.com. PICTURES: Everett Collection Inc / Alamy Images, The Photo Access / Alamy Images, Island Records/Universal Music Group, Hollywood Records Inc/ Disney Music Group.

18-19: WORDS: eonline.com: Corinne Heller, Seventeen.com: Dan Koday, Rollingstone.com: Jason Gay, riaa.com, contactmusic.com. PICTURES: WENN Rights Ltd / Alamy Images, Hollywood Records Inc/ Disney Music Group, Republic Records/Universal Music Group.

20-21: WORDS: Billboard.com: Cathy Applefield Olson, Bustle.com: Caitlyn Callegari, Wikipedia.com. PICTURES: Everett Collection Inc / Alamy Images, WENN Rights Ltd / Alamy Images, AF archive / Alamy Images, Michael Bush / Alamy Images, ZUMA Press, Inc. / Alamy Images.

22-25: WORDS: TVguide.com, Billboard.com: Gary Trust, Wikipedia, Metacritic.com, GMTV, Ellen, MTV.com: Tamar Anitai, Insider.com: Olivia Singh, Rollingston.com: Brittany Spanos. PICTURES: Southcreek Global/ZUMApress.com/ Alamy Images, Paul Smith / Featureflash/ Alamy Images, Nintendo.

26-27: WORDS: Capitalfm.com, The Late, Late Show with James Corden, Chasing Happiness/ Netflix, thethings.com: Caitlyn Fox, Teenvogue.com: Gemma Hartley, Jimmy Fallon, Twitter: Behind the tweets, Eonline.com: Corrine Heller, Seventeen.com: Dan Koday, Westworld.com: Michael Roberts. PICTURES: Lev Radin/Pacific Press/Alamy Images, Jeff Moore/ZUMA Press/ Alamy Images, Republic Records/ Universal Music.

28-29: WORDS: Hollywoodreporter.com: Jocelyn Vena, Mailonline, Forbes.com: Dan Schwabel, Hugh McIntyre, Bustle.com Kyala Hawkins, businessinsider.com: Alyson Shontell, latimes.com: Lauren Beale. PICTURES: Derek Storm/Everett Collection/Alamy Images, Greg Endries/ E!/ Everett Collection/ Alamy Images, Bravo/ NBCUniversal, Phillymack Games.

30-31: PICTURES: Hollywood Records/ Disney Music Group, Republic/ Universal Music Group.

32-33: WORDS: Cosmopolitan.com: Alanna Lauren Greco, Capitalfm.com, Time.com: Mahita Gajanan, Imnsider.com: Kim Renfro and Olivia Singh, Harpersbazaar.com: Amy Mackelden. PICTURES: Everett Collection Inc / Alamy Images, WENN Rights Ltd / Alamy Images, Cronos / Alamy Images, Image Press Agency / Alamy Images.

34-35: WORDS: Celebrity-gossip.net, MTV.com: Amber Katz, Jocelyn Vena, Celebuzz.com, Wikipedia, Hollywoodreporter.com: Shirley Halperin. PICTURES: Tsuni / USA / Alamy Images.

36-37: WORDS: Wikipedia, USmagazine.com, Cosmopolitan.com: Alanna Lauren Greco, Buddytv.com: Meghan Carlson, OCregister.com: Steven Herbert, ibtimes.com: Rachael Ellenbogen. PICTURES: WENN Rights Ltd / Alamy Images, Gregorio T. Binuya, Everett Collection Inc / Alamy Images, Everett Collection Inc / Alamy Image, Eric McCandless / © Disney Channel / Courtesy Everett Collection Inc / Alamy Images.

38-39: WORDS: We Love Pop Magazine: Malcolm Mackenzie, Vulture.com, Rollingstone.com: Brittany Spanos, GQ.com: Eleanor Halls. PICTURES: WENN Rights Ltd / Alamy Images, MediaPunch Inc / Alamy Images, Stranger Things/ Netflix, Columbia Records/ Sony Music Entertainment.

40-41: WORDS: We Love Pop Magazine: Malcolm Mackenzie, Cosmopolitan.com: Kathy Landoli, Rollingstone.com: Brittany Spanos, GQ, who.co.au: Cynthia Wang. PICTURES: MediaPunch Inc / Alamy Images, EDB Image Archive / Alamy Images, Republic/ Universal Music Group, Hollywood Records/ Disney Music Group, The Voice Australia/Talpa Media/ Nine Entertainment Co/ Shine Australia.

42-43: WORDS: Variety.com: Addie Morfoot, MTV, thelondonpaper: Malcolm Mackenzie. PICTURES: ZUMA Press Inc / Alamy Images, WENN Rights Ltd / Alamy Images.

44-45: WORDS: Collider.com: Christina Radish, Buzzfeed.com: Jarett Wieselman, Rollingstone.com: Claire Shaffer, Deadline.com: Anthony D'Allesandro. PICTURES: Starz Digital Media /Courtesy Everett Collection/ Alamy Images,Sony/ Moviestore collection Ltd / Alamy Images, Fox Broadcasting Co/ Jill Greenberg/FOX/ PictureLux / The Hollywood Archive / Alamy Images, Nicole Wilder/ DirecTV TV/courtesy Everett Collection/ Alamy Images, Lionsgate/Entertainment Pictures/ Alamy Images.

46-47: WORDS: Independent.ie/ People.com, B96.cbslocal.com: J Niice, Wikipedia.com. PICTURES: WENN Rights Ltd / Alamy Images.

48-49: PICTURES: Everett Collection Inc / Alamy Images, ZUMA Press, Inc. / Alamy Images, Newscom / Alamy Images, UPI / Alamy Images, Storms Media Group / Alamy Images, Mjt/AdMedia/ZUMA Wire/Alamy Images.

50-51: WORDS: Chasing Happiness/ Amazon Prime Video. PICTURES: Billy Bennight/AdMedia via ZUMA Wire/ Alamy Images, Entertainment Pictures / Amazon Prime Video/ Alamy Images.

52-53: PICTURES: ZUMA Press, Inc. / Alamy Images, Allstar Picture Library / Alamy Images, WENN Rights Ltd / Alamy Images, Everett Collection Inc / Alamy Images, Sppider / Alamy Images, Newscom / Alamy Images.

54-55: PICTURES: Columbia/ Sony Music Entertainment, Hollywood Records/ Disney Music Group, Republic Records/ Universal Music Group.

56-57: PICTURES: WENN Rights Ltd / Alamy Images, dpa picture alliance / Alamy Images, ZUMA Press, Inc. / Alamy Images, Tsuni / USA / Alamy Images, Everett Collection Inc / Alamy Images.

58-61: WORDS: Twitter, The Late, Late Show with James Corden, Variety.com: Michele Amabile Angermiller, billboard.com: Larry Trust, MTV.com: Larry Hosken, Billboard.com: Xander Zellner, Eonline.com: Stephanie Wenger, Accessonline.com, Metro.co.uk: Isla Williams, Wonderlandmagazine.com: Elly Watson. PICTURES: SOPA Images Limited / Alamy Images, imageSPACE/MediaPunch/ Alamy Images, PictureLux / The Hollywood Archive / Alamy Images, The Late Late Show/ CBS Corporation, Republic Records/ Universal Music Group.

62-63: WORDS: Buzzfeed.com: Lauren Yapalater, MTV.com: Patrick Hosken, The Tonight Show/ MTV.com: Jordyn Tilchen, Elle.com: Olivia Blair, Wikipedia, We Love Pop Magazine. PICTURES: Tsuni / USA / Alamy Images.

Back cover PICTURES: PictureLux / The Hollywood Archive / Alamy Images.